The Path Through
A Book of Paintings and Poetry on the Subject of Trauma
By Judith Brassard Brown and Ezra Michael Pryor

First Edition
House of Algos, Inc.

All text and images copyright © 2023 Judith Brassard Brown and Ezra Michael Pryor
Printed in the United States of America
No part of this book may be used or reproduced in any manner without
the written permission except for quotations for review purposes only
ISBN 978-1-7372180-2-9

Design by Scott Ferguson

The Path Through

A Book of Paintings and Poetry on the Subject of Trauma

**Paintings by Judith Brassard Brown
and Poetry by Ezra Michael Pryor**

*The production of a work of art throws
a light upon the mystery of humanity.*

– R. W. Emerson on Nature

Contents

Page iix	*List of Artwork*
Page xi	*Introduction*
Page xiii	*Artist Statement*
Page 3	Shock and Denial
Page 15	Pain and Guilt
Page 27	Anger and Bargaining
Page 37	Depression
Page 49	Reconstruction and Working Through
Page 63	Acceptance and Hope
Page 76	*Artist's Epilogue*

List of Artwork

Cover	*Apart*, 2018, Mixed Media, 40" x 30"
Page x	*Family Cycle (detail)*, 2012, Mixed Media, 9" x 12"
Page xii	*Self Portrait Somewhere Between,* 2020, Oil, 40" x 30"
Page 4	*Rolling In The Night*, 2023, Mixed Media, 24" x 24"
Page 6	*On the Fall*, 2019, Mixed Media, 60" x 36"
Page 8	*New Arrival*, 2007, Mixed Media, 8" x 10"
Page 10	*The Narrows*, 2019, Oil, 40" x 30"
Page 12	*Struggle to the Rise*, 2019, Mixed Media, 20" x 20"
Page 16	*Over There #4*, 2021, Mixed Media, 40" x 30"
Page 18	*Steadfast*, 2023, Mixed Media, 18" x 12"
Page 20	*Too Late*, 2012, Mixed Media, 6" x 8"
Page 22	*Unforeseen*, 2012, Mixed Media, 20" x 16"
Page 24	*Unwieldy Positions*, 2023, Mixed Media, 10" x 10"
Page 28	*In the Air #4*, 2014, Mixed Media, 24" x 30"
Page 30	*Lost and Damaging*, 2019, Mixed Media, 24" x 30"
Page 32	*Running Red*, 2019, Mixed Media, 24" x 24"
Page 34	*Vessel*, 2023, Mixed Media, 8" x 10"

Page 38	*The Climb To The Rise*, 2021, Oil, 24" x 24"
Page 40	*What Remains #6*, 2019, Mixed Media, 8" x 6"
Page 42	*Where There's Smoke*, 2018, Mixed Media, 60" x 36"
Page 44	*The Struggle Home*, 2023, Mixed Media, 10" x 10"
Page 46	*Dance Under the Night Sky*, 2022, Oil, 24" x 24"
Page 50	*Alone*, 2022, Oil, 24" x 24"
Page 52	*Boys Will Be…*, 2017, Oil, 54" x 38"
Page 54	*Horizon,* 2022, Oil, 60" x 36"
Page 56	*Guardians*, 2016, Mixed Media, 40" x 30"
Page 58	*Coming Home*, 2017, Oil, 40" x 30"
Page 60	*The Warriors*, 2011, Mixed Media, 8" x 10"
Page 64	*Heading Home #4*, 2022, Oil, 30" x 40"
Page 66	*After The Storm*, 2022, Oil, 24" x 24"
Page 68	*In Vulci*, 2010, Mixed Media, 16" x 20"
Page 70	*Dreaming of Nada*, 2022, Oil, 24" x 24"
Page 72	*All the Way Home*, 2011, Oil, 40" x 30"
Page 74	*Secret Garden*, 2023, Oil, 40" x 30"

Family Cycle (detail)

Introduction

When we hear a superhero's origin story, it often begins with a traumatic incident: the death of both parents for Batman, the loss of an entire species and home-world for Superman, lab accidents, being bitten by a radioactive spider, being bombarded with cosmic rays… In the comics, and in a fair amount of literature, for that matter, tragedy is the catalyst for extraordinary abilities and change. My experience of dealing with trauma has given me my superpowers of empathy and compassion.

Working through my particular trauma has catalyzed my journey, one of self-knowledge, healing, and sexual discovery. I've become so at home in these spaces that I see it as my life's work. I spend as much of my day as possible helping people one-on-one as a Life & Intimacy Coach. For me, coaching is a way to be the change I want to see in the world; a way to help people feel more comfortable in their own skin. Ideally, coaching provides people with an opportunity to learn and refine skills of self-management, compassion, attunement, and self-love that can serve them for a lifetime.

I have also written about an approach to developing gender and sexuality acceptance, which I call the Cycle of Radical Sexual Acceptance (RSA). RSA is about bringing compassion, understanding, and acceptance to our own ideas of sexuality and gender. It is a roadmap for self-discovery and acceptance that may lead to a transition to the life you long to live. This book, to me, feels like a companion piece to RSA; a guiding light and a reminder that you are not alone on your journey—a reminder there is indeed a *path through*.

– *Ezra Pryor*

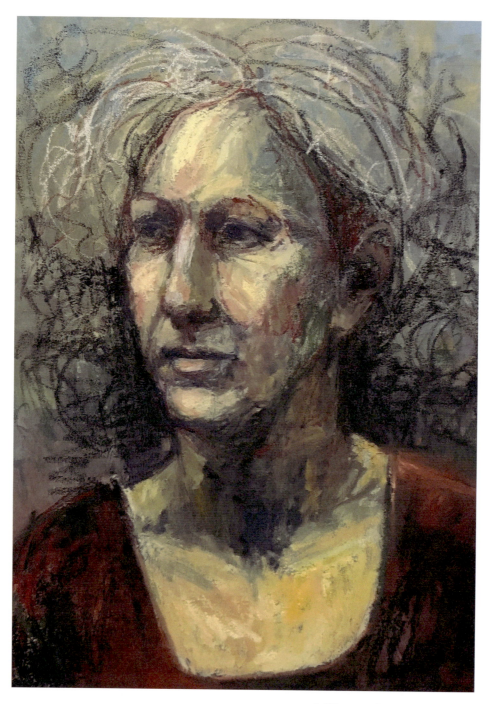

Self Portrait Somewhere Between

Artist Statement

The acts of making and viewing are opportunities to heal. Paintings make connections across time and place, contrast what is seen with what is sensed below the surface. Images and colors in play on the canvas activate connections with others, open doors to buried emotions, take us places we didn't know were there or that we needed to visit. In recognizing what is brought to light, there is the chance we might lighten psychic burdens, find pathways to acceptance, or simple moments of joy.

– Judith Brassard Brown

The Path Through

Shock and Denial

Rolling in the Night

Float

Deafening silence.
My hands and feet are cold,
Dryness in my mouth.
Through a ray of sunlight,
A piece of dust floats downward,
An astronaut untethered.

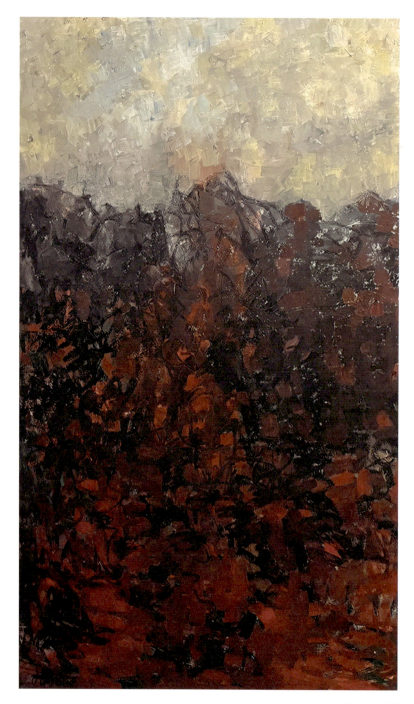

On the Fall

Maybe

The night is quiet,
A storm approaching in the distance.
Perhaps it will never come,
Then I can stay warm and dry.
Maybe I am safe…

New Arrival

Poison

Poison safely locked away,
Where none can reach it.
Keep the lid on tight.
Dark and putrid staring back,
Longing to release its wrath.

The Narrows

Don't

Do not talk about it,
We never do,
And neither should you.
Do not look into its eyes.
Do not run if it follows.
If it touches you,
Hold your scream.

Struggle to the Rise

Martian Scientist

The skin tingles, pins and needles,
An odd but familiar taste.
A cold analytical view comes into focus,
Trying to make sense of it.
Like a strange martian scientist,
Everything seems alien.

Pain and Guilt

Over There #4

Necrotizing

Life at home was like living with a snake with no cage;
Free to roam, lie in wait, strike, envenom.

No one admits it's even there.

I grew weak from bites.
Yet, you all dismissed my pain.

> *It's not that bad, is it?*
> *I'm sorry you feel that way.*
> *That's not how I remember it.*

Fresh venom circulates through my tired veins.

> *Piercing.*
>
> *Paralyzing.*
>
> *Necrotizing.*

Steadfast

Empty

An empty setting,
The hole you left—still bleeding,
Tender, red, and wet.

What could I have done to help?
Would you still be here with me?

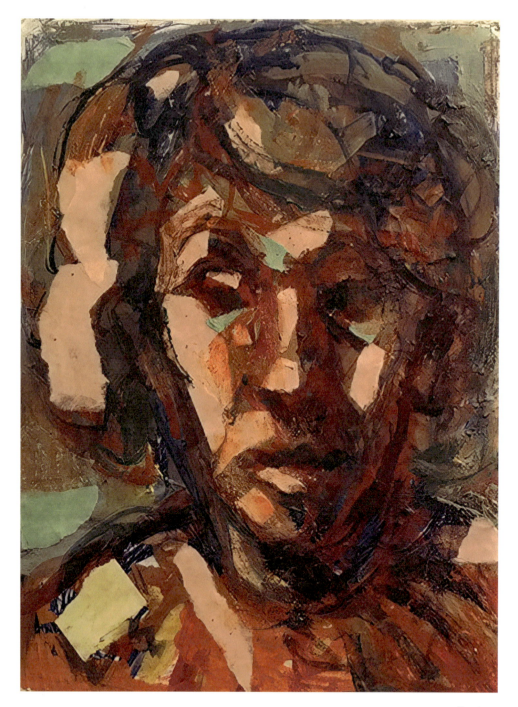

Too Late

it breaks my heart that you can't see my pain

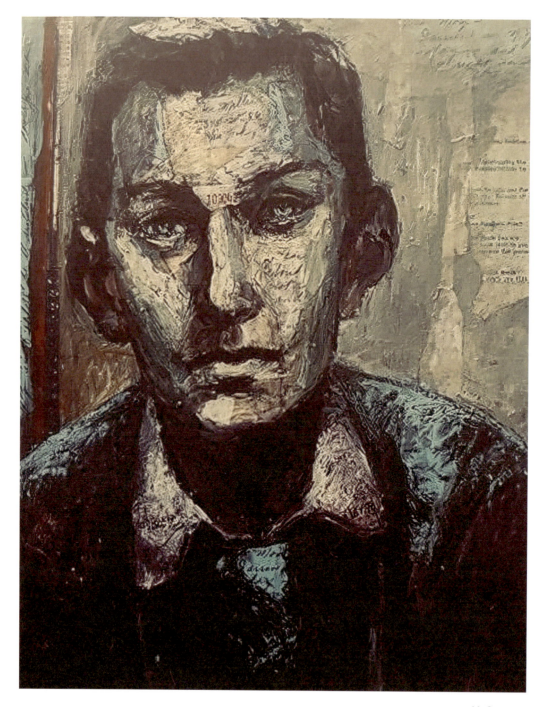

Unforeseen

Before It Was Too Late

I'm sorry I was so angry.
That I missed a chance to be closer before the end.
I know now, it couldn't have been otherwise,
You couldn't have done better.

I wish I could have just been with you,
In peace, before it was too late.
Now, I will never get the chance to say I love you,
And that *everything, even I, will be ok*.

Unwieldy Positions

Lump

All I feel is your absence, piercing,
Like a splinter between my toes,
Pain in every step.
It leaves me feeling sick,
Lightheaded and sweating.
A lump I cannot swallow.

Anger and Bargaining

In the Air #4

Debt

You betrayed me deeply, and now,
I have to pay the debt,
Left to you by your father.
I shouldn't have to do this,
It could have been so different…

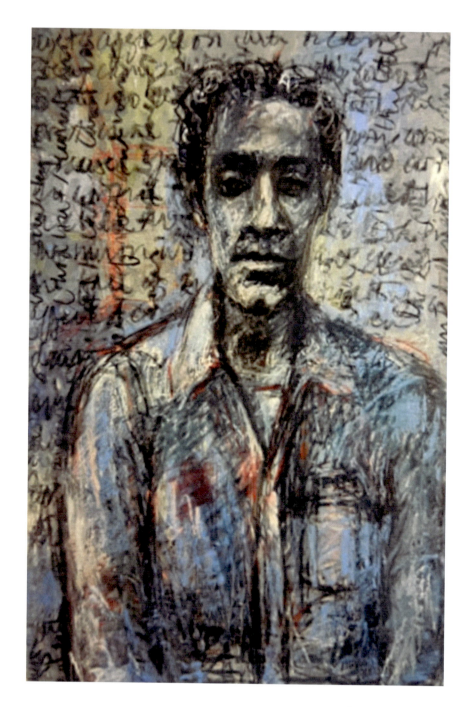

Lost and Damaging

Decimation

FUCK YOU and your whole existence!
Fire is too good for you, a bullet is too quick.
Your suffering should be as protracted as mine has been.
You should swallow hard on the jagged fragments,
Of the teeth I will force from your jaw.

I should beat you to within an inch of your life,
Let you heal and give you hope to live a life again,
Only to decimate your smile.
You should gaze upon your entrails in disbelief,
And bleed out, you *motherfucking monster!*

Running Red

Burning Gaze

Heat radiates from behind my eyes,
Like a burning red laser.
Skin flush, jaw tight,
Daggers for teeth,
Razors for words,
Venom from my lips.

Burning.

Etching.

Contaminating.

Vessel

Whose Anger

This anger,
This heartbreak,
This loneliness,
It is not mine.

Sometimes it looks,
Like it was my father's,
But it's not his either.

Perhaps it could be,
His father's.

It's not me.
Just a feeling,
Like a summer storm passing through,
Making lots of noise on the way,
And leaving hardly a sprinkle.

Depression

The Climb To The Rise

Ash and Cinder

The quiet of the night is punctuated,
By the crackling of burning wood.
Embers streak upward into the inky sky.

Blackness of charred rubble marks our skin,
Searching for something that remains.
But all is lost…

All is ash and cinder.

What Remains #6

Stuck in the Swamp

Knee deep in mud.
The going, slow, the mist, thick.
Small, gnarled trees,
I can't see the edge,
Going on in all directions.

As I lift one foot the other sinks,
Mud coats my skin like tar.

The mud begs to envelop my body,
That I might contribute to its mass,
—*Its stench*.

I could stay here forever,
In the quiet muck.
Peaceful in its own way,
—*Isolated*.

Where There's Smoke

Rain of Ashes

Ashes rain, slowly,
From the black of the night sky.

Flames burn, dimly in the distance,
Shrouded by cloaks of soot.

What remains is yet unknown,
Daylight will show the loss.

The Struggle Home

Dark Purple

Of course she died,
there is no stage five.
For days, I couldn't feel the loss.
Then, like a dark purple shock wave,
It hit me all at once.

I kept apologizing for being so cold,
For being numb while others suffered.
I'll never see her smile again,
I'll never hear her laugh.
No evening singing songs by the piano,
Not another meal at the table together.
Her story is over,
A bright star has gone dim.

Dance Under the NIght Sky

L'Appel Du Vide

Standing at the ledge,
Adrenaline icing my veins,
My mouth dry, my hair,
Standing on end.

I am taunted with images of how my body,
Would spin and tumble on the way down,
The sound it would make against the rocks.

Gripping the tree, I pull myself back,
Then sinking down to scuttle away,
Back to solid ground.

Reconstruction and Working Through

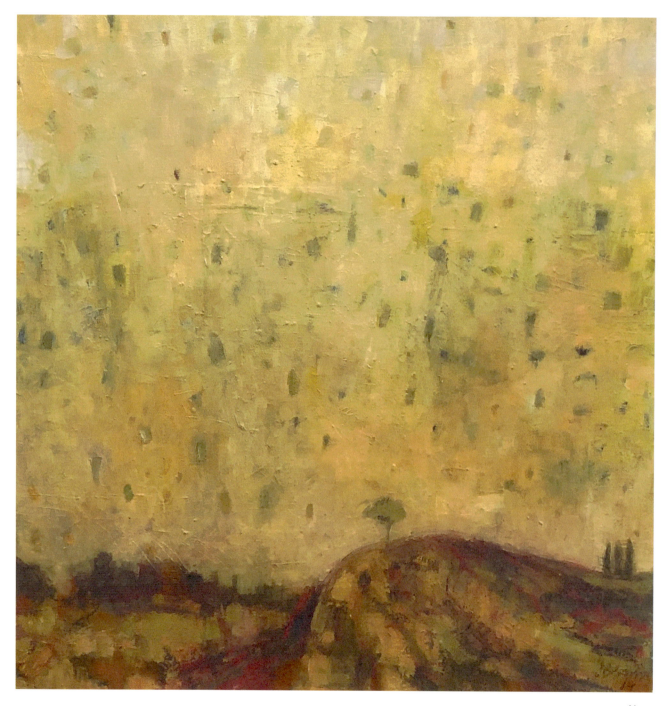

Alone

Family

I'm done being nice,
Bending for your comfort.
I have no desire to punish you,
But if you're tortured by my truth,
I will not be moved.
You may think I'm still angry,
But I'm just over it,
Indifferent.

You say we are family,
And that will always be true,
But we are not *friends*,
And I don't think we ever will be.

Boys Will Be…

Talk With My Son, Bodhi

Come sit with me, there's something I want to talk to you about. I'm going through a tough time but it's getting better. I was hurt, when I was very young, and it is causing me challenges today. It's like my emotions are sick. Like the same bad day keeps repeating over and over.

I'm growing in my awareness, my ability to care for myself, and heal. I'm letting go of so much anger and it's such a relief.

I feel that I have disrespected you in ways my father disrespected me. I am sorry and I want to do better.

I don't want to hurt your feelings, but I know that sometimes I do. I get the instinct to dig my heels in and fight, but it doesn't have to be a fight. I don't want to fight with you, I want to be on your team. I'm on team Bodhi!

Horizon

I'm going to do my best to be present, responsible, and respectful. I know you want to tell me "It's fine" or pat me on the back, but that's not what I need from you now.

What I need is for you to keep standing up to me the way you already do. Just like when you didn't like me calling you my "Baby Boy." I should not have argued with you, you were right. How I refer to you is your choice and I want to respect that. I want to be respectful of your boundaries and in that moment, I wasn't.

I want you to know that if I hurt your feelings or leave you feeling disrespected, that I have made a mistake. You can help me understand how you feel and I can try again to do better. That would help me stay accountable to you.

Thank you for your patience and listening. I'm doing my best and every day I am working to do even better.

Love, Your Father, Ezra

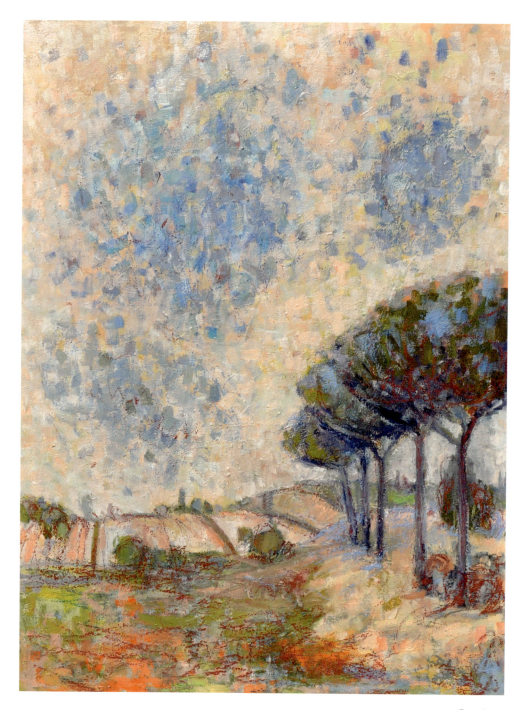

Guardians

Growth

The leaves rattle and buzz a sweet song.
The tree trunk is thicker than I remember.
Branches reaching skyward imparting,
Shade where before, there was none.
A nest held high,
Cradles promises of new beginnings,
Of fresh tomorrows.

Coming Home

Different

Those last steps to the front door always feel the sweetest.
Moments away from kicking off dusty shoes,
From grabbing a cool glass of water and a seat.

Moments away from the shade and quiet of home,
Punctuated by the relentless patter of little bare feet,
On cold terracotta tiles, worn to matte by generations.

Fresh oranges burst with aroma,
As the knife slices through.
Half-toothed smiles and delicious juice,
Shared laughs and hugs.

Different, but not broken,
Not broken, just different.

Warriors

Steadfast

I stand strong and proud,
I am firm in my resolve,
Resilient, steadfast.

No one can discourage me,
The young ones,
Will be kept safe.

Acceptance and Hope

Heading Home #4

Job Well Done

Sunshine warms the wheat.
Earthy fragrance fills the air.
Cicadas singing a familiar song,
As the cool shade invites me:
Come and rest in the warm breeze.
Satisfied, a job well done.

After The Storm

The Road Ahead

The sky is clearing.
The road stretches out ahead.
Leaves wave in the wind,
Beckoning me to move on,
To see what lies ahead.

In Vulci

The Promise of Bread

Gusts of wind dancing upon,
Tips of golden grains.
Wheat bowing and whispering,
The promise of fresh loaves,
Steaming on the dinner table.

Dreaming of Nada

Summer Rain

I can feel you with me,
In the sweet aroma of the sycamore,
In the sound of heavy summer rain,
In the cool grass between my toes,
In the vibrato of Pavarotti in Pagliacci.

I can feel you in the boldness of hope,
In the flowing of tears when the dam breaks.
I can feel you in the quiet moments of peace,
When the clouds begin to break and,
The sun reaches through to touch wet earth.

All the Way Home

Sweet Unknown

Ahead the unknown.
A sweet mystery, unseen,
I yearn to know it.
Somehow, I feel its goodness,
Full of opportunity.

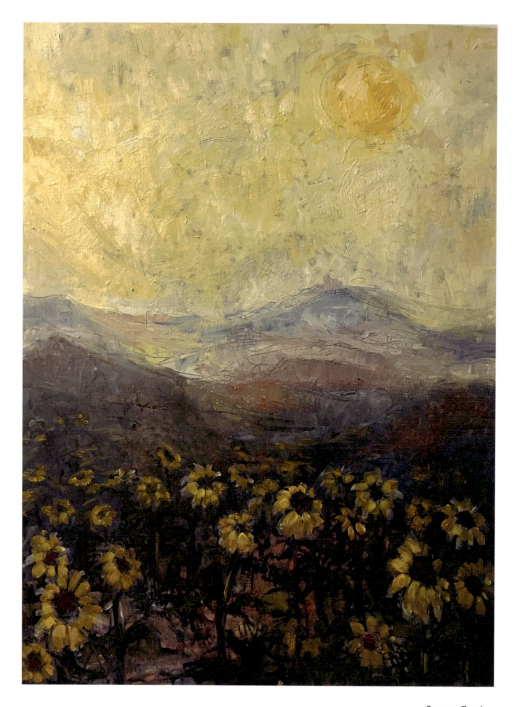

Secret Garden

Smoke In The Maloca

Vine is crawling up my arm,
Here to tell me nothing's wrong.

Phyllis, Nada, Grandpa Norm,
They don't have a body more.

Not below or up above,
All that ever lasts is love.

No need to feel so alone,
They are waiting all at home.

Nothing off or left to do,
They just say I love you too.

Epilogue

When Ezra and I first discussed this project, I was both excited and overwhelmed with how this book could develop. Given that generational trauma is so complex, nuanced, and multilayered, it can feel like an impossible tangle. Each of our traumas involve any combination of family relationships, illness, war, racism, neglect, deprivation, abuse, loss, or other influences. While particulars matter to each of us, what we all have in common is how trauma builds on trauma, impacts our ability to process our experiences, stay balanced, calm, and present. If we are able to acknowledge and do the work to heal, we learn new ways of coping, foster compassion for ourselves and others.

The bare bones of my story sound like soap opera. The death of my grandmother when I was four coincided with sexual abuse in an environment where it was your job to take care of yourself, even as a small child. In an attempt to feel safe, to create a secure home life, I married my first boyfriend soon after college. He was fiercely protective, brilliant in his way and from a very dysfunctional family. He, in turn, felt safe and loved with me. In his mid-twenties, while battling his own mental health issues, he found a way to end it when he committed suicide at the age of twenty-six.

Somehow, I managed to survive. With the help of family and friends, with therapy, I made my way, informed by what I'd learned, as I coped with my experiences. I resolved to do better, to never do that to others. Like so many others, I was determined to prevent harm, or protect, or give care where and whenever I could. While the lessons I'd learned through my own traumas sharpened my vision in some ways, it obscured it in others. It is humbling to see now what I couldn't before and the impact I have had on others.

Painting has been an integral part of the progress I've made, a parallel to the therapy and personal work. Both have been worth the discomfort and persistence. I am grateful making art has been healing both in the process of making and in the paintings themselves. But just as my art practice has changed over time, new approaches and trauma therapies have developed over the years. I wondered whether it was worth the time and energy to begin EMDR in my sixties but investing in this new form of therapy has helped in ways I never could have imagined. Still, I wonder about and mourn the debts I have left for others as I've made my way, debts I can never truly understand or repay.

Lliterature and the arts seem to inform this human struggle, help us learn, heal, or reflect. Painting, like poetry, is a critical way to make meaning, understand and share our lives. Images have a power for emotional healing akin to dreams, giving us space to see, hear, and feel. Wherever you find yourself, from the darkest moments to those of joy and acceptance, I hope these poems and paintings bring some comfort or consolation on the way as you find the courage and strength to stay the course.

– Judith Brassard Brown

2020

Made in the USA
Columbia, SC
29 January 2024